I KNOW AMERICA

Our Money

Karen Bornemann Spies

THE MILLBROOK PRESS

Brookfield, Connecticut

Published by The Millbrook Press
2 Old New Milford Road
Brookfield, CT 06804
© 1992 Blackbirch Graphics, Inc.

Created and produced in association with Blackbirch Graphics.
Series Editor: Bruce S. Glassman

Library of Congress Cataloging-in-Publication Data
Spies, Karen Bornemann.
    Our money / Karen Bornemann Spies
    (I know America)
    Includes bibliographical references and index.
    Summary: A brief overview of the history of money precedes a description
of its minting and use in the United States.
        ISBN 1-56294-212-3 (lib. bdg.)   ISBN 1-56294-815-6 (pbk.)
        1. Money—United States—History—Juvenile literature. [1. Money.] I.
Title. II. Series.
HG501.S75   1992
332.4'973—dc20   91-43231
                                                                              CIP
                                                                               AC

Acknowledgments and Photo Credits

Cover: ©Chuck Peterson; back cover, p. 11 (bottom): Architect of the
Capitol; pp. 4, 6, 7, 10 (bottom), 13: North Wind Picture Archives;
pp. 8, 20: Library of Congress Collection; pp. 10 (upper left), 11 (top),
15, 30, 42: ©Douglas A. Mudd/Smithsonian Institution, National
Museum of American History, National Numismatic Collection;
p. 12: National Portrait Gallery, Smithsonian Institution; p. 16:
©Richard Glassman; pp. 21, 23, 38: ©Stuart Rabinowitz; pp. 26, 33,
34, 36: Bureau of Engraving and Printing, U.S. Treasury; pp. 31, 32:
Official United States Mint Photographs; p. 40: ©Ron Edmonds/AP/
Wide World Photos; p. 45: The Bettmann Archive.

Photo Research by **Inge King.**

10 9 8 7 6 5 4 3 2 1

CONTENTS

THE MEANING
OF MONEY

Imagine that you are stranded on a desert island with a million dollars. How much is it worth? You can't eat it. You have nothing to spend it on. Basically, your money has no value. But once you are rescued, your money immediately becomes very valuable. Why? Because it can buy a lot.

How can money be worthless one minute and valuable the next? What is money anyway? Money is an easy way for people to trade one thing for another. Another name for money is *currency*. Currency refers to both coins and paper money.

How did people get things before currency was invented? Mostly, they traded something they had for

Opposite:
Coinmakers in the Middle Ages cut and stamped gold and silver to make coins.

5

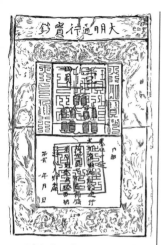

This bank note from the Chinese Ming Dynasty is an early form of paper currency.

something else they wanted. This was known as bartering. For example, let's say a blacksmith made tools and a farmer raised cows. If the farmer needed a tool and the blacksmith wanted a cow, then bartering worked well. But what if the blacksmith wanted a cow, but the farmer didn't need any new tools? Then the blacksmith would have to search for someone else who wanted tools and who had something that the farmer would take for a cow. Bartering became impractical. Besides, it was hard to "make change" with a cow.

Early Kinds of Money

In most early civilizations one or two things came to be used like money. Sometimes it was a useful item such as salt. In other places, common everyday items that may sound odd today were considered to be valuable. For example, fishhooks, human skulls or teeth, and feathers have all been used as "money" at one time or another. Until the 1940s, people on the South Pacific islands of Yap used giant round stones as money. The larger the stone, the more it was worth. Some stones were as large as truck tires and weighed more than a hundred pounds!

Gradually, it became common to trade precious metals for goods. Bronze or gold was shaped into crude bars (ingots). Large bronze or gold pieces were worth more than small ones. Unfortunately, it was hard to tell how much more they were worth. Each

Early Roman money was made out of copper and was cut into pieces about twice this size.

individual piece had to be weighed one at a time to determine its value.

Eventually, precious metals such as gold and silver were made into small disks, or coins. The earliest known coins were made in Asia Minor (now modern day Turkey) about 700 B.C. by the people from a region called Lydia.

Paper Instead of Metal

No matter what metals the coins were made of, carrying a lot of them was difficult. Imagine buying a house and paying for it with coins! That is why paper money was invented. It was first used in China in the thirteenth century. The famous explorer Marco Polo first reported that the emperor Kublai Khan printed notes on mulberry paper.

Our currency system today still uses a mix of coin and paper money. Many people now also use checks and credit cards to purchase goods and services. Whatever forms of money we use today, they are definitely easier than trading tools for cows.

CHAPTER 2

WAMPUM AND SHINPLASTERS

When European settlers first came to North America, they brought their own coins. However, to trade with the Native Americans, the settlers had to use Native American money—wampum, or tiny shells. Strings of shells were cut into six-foot lengths known as fathoms. An earthenware pot for cooking or storing food was worth one fathom. A good deerskin cost two fathoms. Wampum was *legal tender* (a lawful form of money) in the colonies until 1701.

Early Colonial Money

Some of the colonies made their own coins. The Massachusetts Bay Colony opened a mint in Boston in 1652. The mint made Pine Tree shillings until 1686.

Opposite:
English explorers traded goods with Indians from the islands of the West Indies.

The silver Pine Tree shilling was made in Massachusetts between 1652 and 1686.

The colonists also used foreign gold and silver coins. Great Britain owned the colonies, so British pounds, shillings, and pence were common. Pirates and Spanish explorers used Spanish coins to purchase supplies and luxury goods in the colonies.

The First American Paper Money

American paper money first appeared in 1775. The colonies were fighting with Great Britain. One way to show their independence was to issue their own money. It was known as Continental Currency. The value of this money was backed up by a supply of gold. Since gold is always valuable, it is commonly used to "insure" the value of money. Unfortunately, the Continental Congress did not have enough coins or gold to back up all the bills it printed. The bills lost their value. That is why colonists said any worthless thing was "not worth a Continental."

Early American paper money from the Revolutionary War.

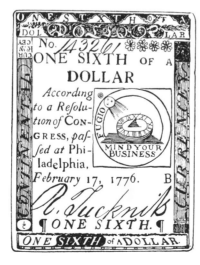

America's first national coin was made from copper in 1787.

The government stopped making the Continental Currency in 1781. But the new nation still needed a national currency system. Members of the Congress wanted American money to be admired and respected throughout the world.

The first national coins were made in 1787. They were copper one-cent coins decorated with a chain of thirteen links. The links circled the words "We Are One." On September 11, 1789, Alexander Hamilton was appointed as the first secretary of the Treasury. Under his leadership, new steps were taken to create public credit for citizens. His reports and many other programs did much to create a sound monetary system for a young United States.

The Coinage Act

In 1792, Congress passed the Coinage Act. It adopted the dollar as our standard monetary unit. The Coinage

Alexander Hamilton served as the first secretary of the U.S. Treasury.

David Rittenhouse served as the first director of the U.S. Mint.

Act also established our country's first mint, located in Philadelphia, to produce the coins. The prominent scientist and astronomer David Rittenhouse was appointed as the first director of the U.S. Mint.

The new mint was only a few hundred feet from President Washington's home. The first coins minted were half dimes. They were made from household silver donated by George and Martha Washington.

All the new coins showed either the head or full figure of a woman who represented Liberty. This was a symbol of American independence. Most European coins at the time had portraits of kings and queens on

SHELL OUT THE BUCKS!

Cabbage, fin, sawbuck. They're all terms for money. What do they mean? Where did they come from?

Buck: A $1 bill. Probably came from the custom of using buckskins as money.

Fin: A $5 bill. Fin is short for *finf*, the Yiddish word for five.

Greenbacks: Paper money. The term was first used in the Civil War, and refers to the green ink used to print the backs of the bills.

Hard money: Coins.

Lettuce or **cabbage**: Paper money. Refers to the green color.

Pin money: Extra cash. Came from the allowance given to women in colonial times to spend on pins. Pins were scarce and expensive. As pins became more plentiful, women spent the money on other things.

Sawbuck: A $10 bill. Related to the use of "buckskins" as money; probably meaning a group of skins or an exceptionally valuable skin.

Shelling out: To pay. Comes from the wampum shells Native Americans used for money.

Soft money: Paper currency. Also called folding money.

Two bits: Slang name for a quarter. *Four bits* is a half dollar. First used in colonial times, when colonists cut Spanish gold coins ("pieces of eight") to make change. Half a coin was "four bits," and a quarter section was "two bits."

Trading with buckskins

them. President Washington did not want his likeness on any American coins. He thought it would look as if he were trying to be a king.

The United States government did not issue paper money until the Civil War. Until then, paper money was printed by private companies and state banks. Pennsylvania alone issued 250 different kinds of bills. Massachusetts had thirteen different kinds. But when the war came, a great deal of money was needed to finance it. So the government began to print "greenbacks." This nickname came from the green ink that was used to print the back side of the bills. Greenbacks were worth less than their face value (amount printed on the front). In other words, if you turned in a five dollar bill to the government during the Civil War, you would have received less than five dollars worth of gold.

Shinplasters and Confederate Money

Because people hoarded coins, there weren't enough to make change. The government issued tiny bills known as fractional currency. They were about the size of postage stamps. They were printed in denominations of 3 cents, 5 cents, 10 cents, 15 cents, 25 cents, and 50 cents. These small bills were also called *shinplasters*. Soldiers used them to line their shoes and wrap their shins to keep out the cold.

During the Civil War, the Confederacy issued its own currency as a way to emphasize the strong

independence of the Southern states. These notes were good only in states that had seceded from the Union.

After the Civil War, the United States was united again under one government. Paper money became more valuable. For every dollar in paper money, the United States owned an equal amount of gold bullion (gold bars). Beginning in 1865, the government began printing pieces of paper money known as gold certificates. These certificates could be exchanged for gold bullion. Gold certificates continued to circulate (were in use) until 1933.

Silver certificates were first issued in 1878. They could be exchanged for silver dollars or silver bullion. By the late 1960s, there was a worldwide shortage of silver. For this reason, the government stopped circulating silver certificates in 1968. They were replaced by Federal Reserve Notes, which are still in use today.

3

WHO'S ON A $100 BILL?

Do you know who or what is pictured on our paper money? Can you describe what is stamped on each U.S. coin? This chapter answers these questions.

Current Types of U.S. Bills

There are two kinds of paper money in circulation. Both United States notes and Federal Reserve notes are legal tender for paying bills and debts.

Federal Reserve Notes

Federal Reserve notes make up about ninety-nine percent of all paper money in circulation. They are issued by the Federal Reserve Bank in denominations

Opposite:
The Federal Reserve Board Building is in Washington, D.C. The Federal Reserve controls the supply of money in the United States.

$1, $2, $5, $10, $20, $50, and $100. Some $500, $1,000, $5,000, and $10,000 bills are still circulated today, but none have been printed since 1945.

United States Notes

United States notes were the country's first national paper currency. They were originally issued in 1862 in these denominations: $1, $2, $5, $10, $20, $50, $200, $500, $1,000, $5,000, and $10,000. Today United States notes make up only a small part of the paper money in circulation. They are issued only in the $100 denomination. At some point, they will no longer be used, since they serve the same purpose as the newer Federal Reserve notes.

What's Printed on Our Paper Money?

Each denomination has a unique portrait of a famous American on the front. Each back also has its own individual design. The $100 and $50 bills have a new design. Eventually, all denominations will have the new design. All bills, however, are printed with certain items in common.

Serial Numbers and Star Notes

Each note has its own eight-digit serial number which appears twice on the face, or front of the note. A serial number includes a letter in front of it and another after it (serial numbers on the new bills have two letters in front), except for serial numbers on "star" notes. A star

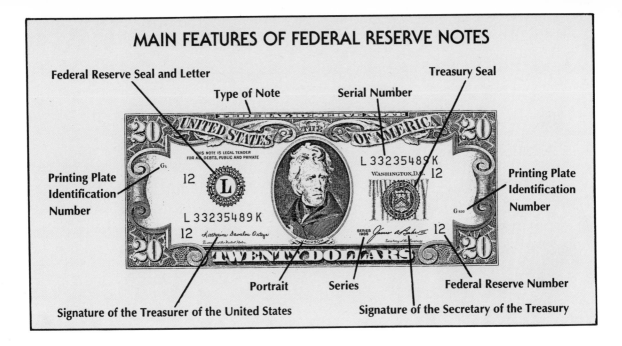

MAIN FEATURES OF FEDERAL RESERVE NOTES

note replaces a regular note that has been damaged in printing. It is just like the note it replaces except for the star, which is substituted for one of the serial letters.

Series

All paper money bears a series identification. The series date shows the year in which each bill was reprinted. The first letter in the serial number of the new bills shows the series; the letter A stands for 1996.

Treasury Seal

This seal has been on every piece of United States paper money since 1862. It includes a key, which stands for safety, and scales, which stand for justice. The Treasury Seal, or "stamp of approval," shows that the bill is legal tender. It appears in several different forms and colors, depending on the bill's denomination.

The Great Seal of the United States

The Great Seal was adopted in 1782 and now appears on the back of the $1 bill. The seal shows the bald eagle, our national bird. A shield with vertical stripes and a wide bar across the loop—the arms of the United States—is on its chest. Above the eagle are thirteen stars, which stand for the thirteen original colonies. The eagle holds a ribbon printed with the motto *E pluribus unum* ("Out of many, one"). On the seal back, at the left side of the bill, is an image of an unfinished pyramid, a symbol of strength. Above the pyramid is the "all-seeing eye of God" inside a triangle. At the base of the pyramid are the Roman numerals for 1776, the date of our nation's birthday. Around the edge at the top is a Latin motto, *Annuit coeptis* ("God has favored our undertakings"). On a ribbon at the bottom is another bit of Latin: *Novus ordo seclorum* ("A new order of the ages").

The Great Seal appears on many official U.S. items and documents, including the back of the $1 bill.

"In God We Trust"

The motto "In God We Trust" first appeared on coins during the Civil War. However it was not printed on paper currency until 1957. A determined man named Matt Rothert convinced the government to add the motto to paper money. Rothert wrote more than one thousand letters to government leaders. Finally, his idea became law in 1955.

MONEY MATCHES

The following images appear on U.S. bills:

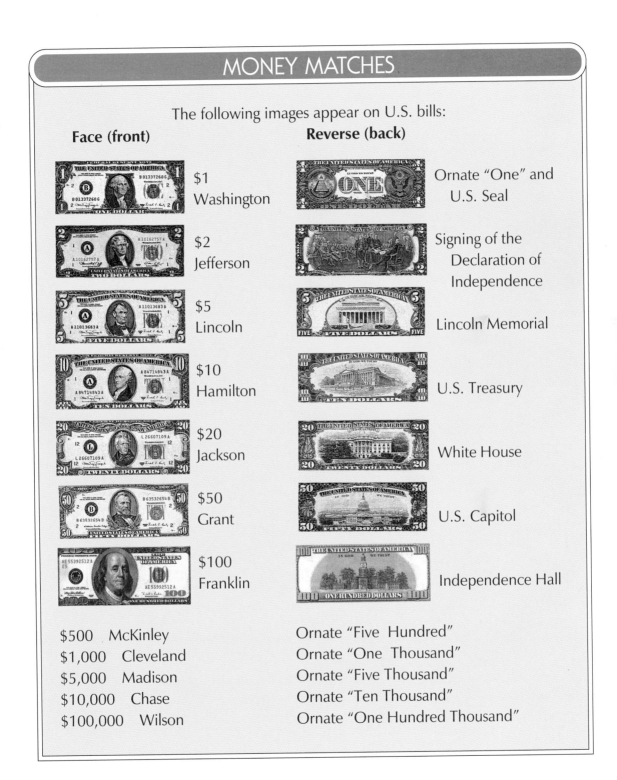

Face (front)	Reverse (back)
$1 Washington	Ornate "One" and U.S. Seal
$2 Jefferson	Signing of the Declaration of Independence
$5 Lincoln	Lincoln Memorial
$10 Hamilton	U.S. Treasury
$20 Jackson	White House
$50 Grant	U.S. Capitol
$100 Franklin	Independence Hall

$500	McKinley	Ornate "Five Hundred"
$1,000	Cleveland	Ornate "One Thousand"
$5,000	Madison	Ornate "Five Thousand"
$10,000	Chase	Ornate "Ten Thousand"
$100,000	Wilson	Ornate "One Hundred Thousand"

Signatures, Letters, and Numbers

All paper currency shows the engraved facsimile, or copy, of two signatures. Since 1914, all bills show the signatures of the secretary of the Treasury and of the treasurer of the United States. But different bills may have different signatures. That is because many people have served in these positions over the years.

Bills are printed in sheets, thirty-two at a time. Small letters and numbers show each bill's location on the print sheet. These letters and numbers appear on the front of the bill.

CODING OUR CURRENCY

The United States is divided into twelve Federal Reserve districts. Each Federal Reserve bank is in charge of the currency circulation for its district. A seal printed in black at the left of the portrait gives the name and letter of the Federal Reserve bank that issued it. On the new bills, a universal seal is used to represent the entire Federal Reserve system. A letter and number beneath the left serial number identifies the Federal Reserve bank.

The district numbers, cities, and their matching letter symbols are:

1	Boston	A	7	Chicago	G
2	New York	B	8	St. Louis	H
3	Philadelphia	C	9	Minneapolis	I
4	Cleveland	D	10	Kansas City	J
5	Richmond	E	11	Dallas	K
6	Atlanta	F	12	San Francisco	L

U.S. Coins

Many changes in coin design have been made since 1792, when the Mint was founded. At that time, gold was used in the eagle ($10), half eagle ($5), and quarter eagle ($2.50) pieces. The dollar, half dollar, quarter, dime, and half dime were made of silver. The cent and half cent were made of copper.

In 1933, during the Great Depression, the U.S. Mint stopped producing gold coins. By 1970, silver was

The secretary of the Treasury chooses the designs for paper currency. The designs must have

historical importance. They cannot depict a living person. Different engravers are chosen to do the portraits, letters, borders, and backgrounds.

The designs on today's bills date from 1929, when all bills were changed to the modern small size. The secretary of the Treasury appointed a committee to decide whose pictures should appear on the bills. The committee thought that all the bills should show United States presidents. The secretary of the Treasury changed the committee's decision slightly. Alexander Hamilton was chosen to be on the $10 bill, because he was the first secretary of the Treasury. Benjamin Franklin appears on the $100 bill, because he was a famous statesman and one of the signers of the Declaration of Independence. A picture of Salmon P. Chase was printed on the $10,000 bill. As

secretary of the Treasury during the Civil War, Chase helped develop and oversee the creation of our national banking system.

eliminated from newly minted United States coins. This change was necessary because of the world shortage of silver. Today coins are made of a core of nonprecious metal, such as copper. The core is "clad," or sandwiched between, layers of alloy (two or more metals combined together).

INTERESTING FACTS ABOUT MONEY

★ A stack of currency one mile high would contain over 14.5 million notes.

★ If you had ten billion $1 bills and spent one every second of every day, it would take 317 years for you to go broke.

★ How many times do you think you could fold a dollar bill before it would tear? About four thousand double folds (first forward and then backward) are necessary before a dollar will tear.

★ The largest denomination of paper money ever printed was the $100,000 gold certificate of 1934. It was used only in official bank deals. The largest bill printed for circulation was the $10,000.

★ The Bureau of Engraving and Printing has printed paper currency for the governments of the Philippines, the Republic of Cuba, Thailand, and Korea.

★ The Denver Mint produces one million coins an hour. It costs two thirds of a cent to produce a penny. To make $10 worth of half dollars costs $3.88.

★ The Mint has made coins for China, Costa Rica, El Salvador, Haiti, Honduras, Israel, Liberia, Mexico, and the Philippines.

What's on Each Coin?

Each coin must be stamped with the amount of money it is worth. The word *Liberty* is stamped on coins to remind us that we live in a country that loves freedom. The Latin motto *E pluribus unum* ("Out of many, one") tells that many people joined together to form our nation. The motto "In God We Trust" has appeared on all coins since 1984.

Some coins contain a mint mark. The letter *D* is stamped on coins from the Denver Mint, a *P* means Philadelphia, and an *S* stands for San Francisco.

Who's on Each Coin?

By law the design of coins cannot be changed more often than once every twenty-five years. Most current coins honor U.S. presidents. The Susan B. Anthony dollar coin and the American Bald Eagle dollar coin are two exceptions. The John F. Kennedy half dollar is the most recent coin with a U.S. president. It was introduced in 1964. The Dwight D. Eisenhower dollar is no longer being made, but is still legal tender.

COINING AN IMAGE

The following list shows who is pictured on each coin:

Front

Cent
Abraham Lincoln

Nickel
Thomas Jefferson

Dime
Franklin D. Roosevelt

Quarter
George Washington

Half dollar
John F. Kennedy

Dollar
Dwight D. Eisenhower

Back

Lincoln Memorial

Monticello
(Jefferson's Home)

Torch with olive branch
and oak branch

American Eagle

The Great Seal

Bald eagle with olive
branch

C H A P T E R

MAKING OUR MONEY

The Department of the Treasury has two divisions that prepare all paper money and coins. These divisions are the United States Mint and the Bureau of Engraving and Printing.

The United States Mint

The headquarters of the U.S. Mint is in Washington, D.C. The coins are made in two branches of the Mint, in Philadelphia and Denver. Commemorative coins are made at the San Francisco Mint. Commemoratives honor landmark dates, special people, or events in American history and are very popular among the growing group of coin collectors.

Opposite:
Metal printing plates for a $1 bill cover a press at the Bureau of Engraving and Printing.

Alloy: A combination of two or more metals.

Annealing: The heating process that softens metal.

Blanks: Circles of metal to be made into coins. See planchet.

Bullion: Bars of crudely prepared metal.

Cladding: The process of bonding strips of metal together. Used today in the making of coins.

Die: A device for exactly copying patterned impressions.

Ingot: A mass of metal cast into a bar shape.

Numismatics: The study or collection of currency.

Planchet: A blank coin.

Upsetting machine: The machine that spins blanks. As it spins, the machine puts the raised edges on the coins.

How Coins Are Made

Before a coin begins production, a design must be approved by the secretary of the Treasury. Once a design is final, a model is made from a soft plastilene (modeling wax). Then a plaster of Paris model is made from the plastilene one, with most of the details added. The plaster of Paris model is used to make a final model from epoxy, which is a very hard substance. A special tracing tool transfers the design from the epoxy to a metal blank (a coin with nothing stamped on it). Master printing dies are made from the blank. These dies then imprint the words and pictures onto the finished coins.

Let's go on tour through the Mint and follow the steps in making a coin.

1. A Metal "Sandwich"

Gone are the days of silver and gold coins. Today's coins are made of strips of alloy. The strips are shipped to the Mint from private companies. They weigh about six thousand to eight thousand pounds. The strips are 13 inches wide and 1,500 feet long. That's as long as five football fields.

Dimes, quarters, half dollars, and dollars are made of three layers of metal bonded together like a sandwich. This process is called *cladding.* The top and bottom of the metal "sandwich" is a mixture of three parts copper to one part nickel. The core is pure copper. If you look at the edges of one of these coins, you can see the "sandwich" layers.

Once a coin design is approved, a model of the coin is made from a modeling wax called plastilene. Then a plaster of Paris model is made from the plastilene model. An epoxy model is then made from the plaster of Paris version.

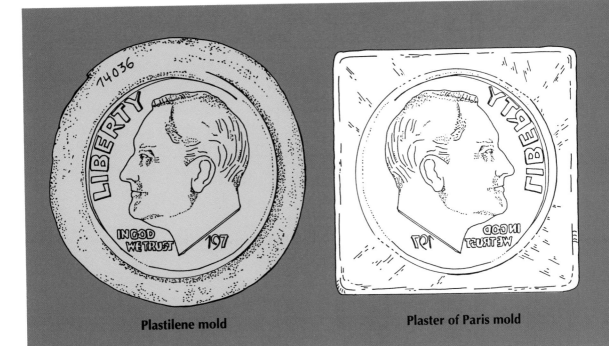

Plastilene mold   Plaster of Paris mold

The strips for nickels are cupronickel—three parts copper and one part nickel. Since 1982, cents have been made of copper-plated zinc. They are cheaper to manufacture and weigh less than copper cents.

2. The "Cookie Cutter"

The metal strips are fed into machines called blanking presses. The presses stretch the metal and cut round blanks (planchets). The leftover punched strips are melted down and made into new ones.

THE UNWANTED COIN

In 1979, a new dollar coin was introduced, the Susan B. Anthony dollar. It honored the famous leader in the women's movement to get the vote. This was the first coin to honor an American woman. It was expected to be a popular coin. But it wasn't.

People refused to use the Susan B. Anthony dollar. They didn't like its size because it was too similar to the other coins. It was smaller than a half dollar and not much larger than a quarter.

The Susan B. Anthony dollar coin

The Mint stopped making these dollars in 1981. About $15 million in Susan B. Anthony coins are stored at the Denver Mint. This is just a portion of the coins stored in government vaults across the United States.

3. Heat, a Bath, and a Shine

The blanks are heated in a very hot oven called an annealing furnace. This softens them and prepares them for stamping. The softened blanks are put in a chemical bath, which cleans and polishes them. Then the planchets are rinsed and dried.

4. Rolled Rims

This process is like putting the edge on a pizza crust. The blanks go into an "upsetting" machine, which spins like a merry-go-round. The spinning pushes the blanks against the edge of the machine. This produces the raised ("upset") rim.

5. Stamping

The planchets are put into a coin press. A ring, or collar, holds each blank in place. Master coinage dies stamp the designs onto the blanks. One heavy blow stamps the coins on each side at the same time.

6. Shaking, Counting, and Weighing

The finished coins pass through a "shaker," which vibrates them. The ones that are too small or too large stay in the shaker. The good coins are then counted by machine and put into bags. The bags are sewn shut by a special machine that looks like a hand-held sewing machine. The bags are weighed before they are stored or shipped. The scales are so accurate that they can tell if a bag is short only one coin!

Dimes, quarters, half dollars, and dollars are put into sacks that each holds $1,000 worth of coins. Nickel sacks hold $200 each, and cents, $50.

The Bureau of Engraving and Printing

All paper money is designed, engraved, and printed at the Bureau of Engraving and Printing in Washington, D.C. The bureau also prints Treasury bonds, U.S. postage stamps, and other important documents.

The Engraving Process

Paper money is printed by the *intaglio* process from engraved plates. First, the different parts of the design are hand-tooled into steel plates. Specially skilled engravers use delicate tools called gravers. For security reasons, each feature on each bill is hand-engraved by a different engraver. Thus, one engraver does the portrait, another does the border, another does the numerals, and so on. Picture engravers must serve as apprentices for ten years before they are

Finished coins are counted and then sewn into bags by a special machine.

allowed to do an actual bill. Letter engravers are apprenticed for seven years.

If you look closely at a bill, you can see the skill and artistry of each engraver. Notice that the portrait is made of many fine lines, dots, and dashes. These vary in size and shape. The use of both heavy and light lines makes counterfeiting a bill very difficult.

The next step in the process is transferring the design from the hand-engraved dies to a printing plate. The original engraved dies are stored. They may be used over again. For example, the Lincoln portrait on the $5 bill was engraved in 1869. It can still be used for printing bills today.

The Printing Process

The bureau prints all paper money on high-speed printing presses. The most modern presses use four plates of thirty-two bills each. They print over eight thousand sheets per hour. That's more than a quarter of a million bills each hour.

Sheets of printed $20 bills roll through a machine before they are inspected and cut.

The bills are printed on specially produced paper. The backs of the notes are printed with green ink. They are allowed to dry for twenty-four to forty-eight hours. Then the faces are printed with black ink and allowed to dry.

Checking, Cutting, and Overprinting

After the printing, each thirty-two-bill sheet is cut in half. It is examined for mistakes. Then a letterpress completes the printing process. The serial number, Treasury seal, and appropriate Federal Reserve district seal and number are printed on the bills.

Special machines cut the notes into individual bills. (Currency printed since 1929 measures 6.14 inches by 2.61 inches.) The bills are then banded into stacks of a hundred. The stacks are packaged into "bricks" of four thousand bills each. The bricks are put in pouches for shipment to one of the Federal Reserve banks.

Counterfeiting

Counterfeiting is forging or making an illegal copy of a coin or bill. Counterfeit coins are less of a problem than counterfeit notes. The Treasury Department has developed ways to make counterfeiting difficult. Each engraver has his or her own special style, which is difficult to copy. Just as it is hard to copy someone's signature, it is hard to copy exactly the style of each engraver. Currency paper is of higher quality than

Inspectors at the
Bureau of Engraving
and Printing care-
fully check each
sheet of money that
is printed.

most other paper. The green ink used is very difficult
to photograph. The shading does not come out clearly,
making it hard for a couterfeiter to copy.

Modern counterfeiters use laser printers and
color copiers to make illegal copies of notes. But the
Treasury Department has already developed two new
ways to protect money.

In one method, polyester colored threads with
the initials *USA* and the denomination are woven into
the bill next to the portrait. Polyester thread cannot be
copied on a color copier. If you hold such a bill up to
the light, you will be able to see these threads. You
will not be able to see them in a counterfeit bill.

In the second, the words *The United States of America* are engraved on the sides of the portrait. The letters are designed to be too small to be copied clearly by a regular photocopy machine.

These measures—security thread and very small printing—have already been added to $100 bills. They will soon be added to all other currency, except for $1 bills, which are not usually worth counterfeiting.

COUNTERFEITERS

Where do counterfeiters come from? They can be from any walk of life. One man from Missouri made $15,000 in counterfeit $10 bills. Yet he had not finished eighth grade.

Counterfeiters hire people to help them pass off fake currency. One way is for a group of money passers to work together. They go into stores at busy periods. They pay for a few dollars' worth of merchandise using a fifty-dollar bill. They get their change in real money. By the time someone notices the counterfeit money, the people who have passed it are many miles away.

The largest counterfeit ring in history was organized by the Nazis during World War II. Adolph Hitler ordered more than $630 million of counterfeit British currency to be made. Men and women began passing this money all over Britain and in other countries where British money was accepted. Hitler hoped that other countries would lose confidence in the British economy. He also wanted to confuse the British people, so that they would lose faith in their government. Hitler believed this would help Germany gain power over Great Britain. However, Germany was defeated by the Allies before the Nazi plan could succeed.

C H A P T E R

5

CIRCULATING
AND COLLECTING
OUR CURRENCY

The Treasury Department ships new paper money and coins to the Federal Reserve banks. The Reserve banks pay it out to commercial banks and savings and loan associations. People get money when they cash checks or withdraw money at their banks. They then spend the money, which is redeposited in banks.

Congress passes laws about the maximum amount of money that can be in circulation at any one time. The Federal Reserve System supervises the flow of money. The president of the United States appoints seven governors of the Federal Reserve Board. They serve for fourteen years. In this way, they can make money decisions that will be good for the country for a long time.

Opposite:
As money circulates, it becomes worn. The average $1 bill lasts only about eighteen months.

When Money Wears Out

As money circulates, it wears out or becomes damaged. The average $1 bill, for example, lasts fifteen to eighteen months. Larger denominations last longer, because they do not circulate as much as the $1 bill. A $20 bill lasts four years, and a $50 lasts nine years. Coins last much longer than paper money. Most circulate for fifteen years.

What should you do if you receive a torn bill? Is it still worth a dollar? A bank will give you an undamaged bill for a torn one. But it must be clearly more than one half of the original note.

The bank then sends your torn bill to a Federal Reserve bank, along with any other damaged money it has collected. The Federal Reserve bank counts the damaged money. It decides if it is "fit" or "unfit" for use. Fit (reusable) money is stored in vaults until it is needed. Unfit currency is destroyed. Damaged and worn coins are returned to the Treasury Department. They are melted down and made into new coins.

What happens if the note is so badly damaged that you cannot tell what it is? What if you have less than half of the bill? Then you have what is known as mutilated currency. Sometimes mutilated currency has been damaged by chemicals, fires, or explosives. Sometimes insects eat

Alan Greenspan was an influential chairman of the Federal Reserve Board during the 1980s and 1990s.

ROB THE MINT?

The Denver Mint seems like a tempting target for robbery. It is a storehouse for tons of coins. More than 50 million ounces of gold bars are stored deep below the Mint. The gold belongs to the United States government and is never sold or used.

Security is tight. Visitors must be X-rayed by equipment similar to that at airports. Employees are not allowed to bring coins into the building. They must use special credit cards to operate the vending machines. All workers are X-rayed before they are allowed to leave the building.

Gold has been stolen just once in the Mint's history. In 1926, an employee with an artificial leg smuggled out $80,000 worth of small gold bars in his hollow limb. He was caught and sent to prison. Security in the Mint was tightened.

The largest theft took place in front of the Mint, not inside it. It is known as the Great Mint Robbery. It took place on December 18, 1922. Brand new, crisp five-dollar bills—$20,000 worth—were being transferred from the Mint into a Federal Reserve bank car. Four bandits with sawed-off shotguns grabbed the money bags. One guard was killed. Twenty-seven days later the getaway car was found locked in a garage near the center of Denver. In the front seat was the frozen body of one of the gang members. He had been shot during the robbery. No further evidence was found and no one was ever charged with the crime.

parts of it. Mutilated currency must be sent to the U.S. Treasury Department. Experts there decide how much it is worth. They redeem the mutilated currency. This means they mail checks back to the people who sent in the damaged money. Every year the Treasury redeems more than $30 million of mutilated currency.

The Fun of Numismatics

The study or collection of coins and paper money is called *numismatics*. Many people enjoy collecting rare coins or bills. "Mistakes" in the printing or coining process become valued collectors' items.

Each year the Mint produces "proof" coins for collectors. Proof coins are made shinier than regular ones by a special polishing process. They are then sealed in plastic.

COLLECTING CURRENCY

If you are interested in learning more about collecting currency, look in your telephone book under "Hobbies" or "Coins." To get ordering information for U.S. Mint coins and medals contact:

Customer Service
  Center
United States Mint
10001 Aerospace
  Drive
Lanham, Maryland
  20706
(301) 436-7400

For more information about collecting special documents and United States paper money contact the Department of the Treasury at:

Public Affairs
  Bureau of Engraving and Printing
Department of the
  Treasury
14th and C Street,
  NW
Room 602-11A
Washington, D.C.
  20228
(202) 447-0193

The Bicentennial Coin
of 1976

Uncirculated mint sets are also packaged each year. They include one of each denomination of coin. Unlike proofs, they are ordinary coins. They have not been specially polished.

From time to time, the Mint produces special coins in honor of historical events or to honor a famous person. The first commemorative coin was minted in 1892 to help finance the World's Columbian Exposition in Chicago. Since that time, the Mint has issued many commemorative coins. They sell for more than the face value, so they rarely circulate.

The Mint also produces commemorative medals. They honor famous people in our country's history. For example, there are bronze medals honoring each American president.

The Bureau of Engraving and Printing also has a mail order sales division. It sells items such as uncut sheets of currency and presidential portraits.

Collecting coins tends to be more popular than collecting paper money. The value of coins depends on their condition. Proof coins or uncirculated sets are worth more than worn coins. The fewer coins of a given type that are minted, the more each one of them is worth. Older coins tend to be worth more than recent issues. For example, the first coins struck at the Mint were silver half cents. Some of them are valued at more than $20,000. Mistakes in printing also raise the value. The 1937 three-legged buffalo nickels are worth $80 to $1,500. Ordinary 1937 nickels are valued at 30 cents to $25.

The Value of Money Today

Thousands of years ago, people could get along without money. They lived on the food they grew and the things they got by bartering. Today the world is very different. We depend on money.

Imagine what would happen if suddenly there were no money. Stores would close. Cars and trains and airplanes couldn't operate. People who lived on farms could at least feed themselves for a while. But how would they buy seeds or animals without money?

Still, some people think there will be no need for money in the future. Electronic bank tellers and facsimile (fax) machines will carry on bank business. Purchases will be done with credit cards or checks. Bills or coins won't be needed.

It is hard to predict how our money system might change in the future. However, we can be sure that the Treasury Department will respond to a need for change. In the past, the Treasury has adapted money to fit our needs. That is why some types of currency are no longer used. We now have plenty of coins, so there's no need for fractional paper currency. When gold and silver each became more scarce, gold and silver certificates were no longer issued. Large-sized bills were replaced by the modern-sized paper currency in 1929. This might sound like a lot of changes, but actually it's not. United States money has been changed the least of any major currency in the world.

The first American money was designed to show our independence from Britain. Then, American leaders worked hard to plan a strong currency system. Today, Congress and the Federal Reserve Board control the amount of money that can be circulated. If the amount in circulation were suddenly doubled, that would mean that the value of the dollar would drop a great deal. The Federal Reserve Board continues as our "money doctor," watching to see when banks need more currency and when they need less. In this way, all American citizens and their money are protected.

In Germany after World War I, the German mark became worthless. Citizens were forced to carry baskets full of money to buy simple items.

45

Chronology

700 B.C.	Earliest known coins made in Asia Minor (modern day Turkey) by people of a region called Lydia.
1652	The Massachusetts Bay Colony opens a mint in Boston, making the Pine Tree Shilling until 1686.
1775	American paper money, called Continental Currency, first appears.
1787	The first national coins, made of copper, are introduced.
1789	Alexander Hamilton is appointed the first secretary of the Treasury.
1792	Congress passes the Coinage Act, adopting the dollar as the standard monetary unit. David Rittenhouse is appointed the first director of the U.S. Mint.
1865	The government begins printing gold certificates.
1878	The first silver certificates are issued.
1968	Circulation of silver certificates ends.
1970	Silver is eliminated from newly minted coins due to worldwide shortages.

For Further Reading

Clinton, S. *Susan B. Anthony.* Chicago: Childrens Press, 1989.

Davis, Bertha. *The National Debt.* New York: Franklin Watts, 1990.

Dunnan, Nancy. *Banking.* Englewood Cliffs: Silver Burdett Press, 1990.

Schlesinger, Arthur M., Jr., ed. *The Department of the Treasury.* Broomall: Chelsea House, 1990.

Schlesinger, Arthur M., Jr., ed. *The Federal Reserve System.* Broomall: Chelsea House, 1990.

Index